T0370133

A LITTLE BOOK

of SELF-CARE

for BRIDES

A LITTLE BOOK

of SELF-CARE

for BRIDES

with a foreword by

SARA K. RUNNELS

FLASH
POINT

Published by Flashpoint™ Books, Seattle
www.flashpointbooks.com

Produced by Girl Friday Productions

Design: Rachel Marek
Production editorial: Abi Pollokoff and Kylee Hayes
Development & editorial: Kristin Duran

Image credits (all credits belong to Shutterstock users): cover, vector_ann (cake); cover, ii–iii, 2, 20–21, 57, 64–65, 80, 82, 87, 93, 101, 106–107, 110, 117, 119, 126, TWINS DESIGN STUDIO (watercolor); v, Reytr; viii, 8, 27, 62, My Ho; 4, 13, 122, Akhmedova Albina; 10–11, 78–79, 112–113, bardockstudio; 14, Sippung; 17, 23, GreenArtStory; 18, Anna Szonn; 24, 67 (left), DreamLoud; 29, 44, Flora And Bear; 33, 69, Atomorfen Illustration; 34–35, 124–125, Liska Art; 39, Naticka; 40, morevaart; 46–47, Hybrid_Graphics; 50, Katerina Tyshkovskaya; 53, Eva Kleinman; 54, Lyubov Zaytseva; 67 (right), Irina_Russkikh; 70, lichu; 74, Mariia Kutuzova; 91, IFofito; 97, Annet Kuzmina; 98, cuteaspushkin; 103, Leamila; 109, darina.ill; 111, VerisStudio; 116, Shilovka; 127, Artloca; 128 and 129, KutuzovaDesign and Bogomolova Irina; 130, ArtCreationsDesignPhoto; 134, PYRAMIS

ISBN (hardcover): 978-1-964721-11-8
ISBN (ebook): 978-1-964721-12-5

Library of Congress Control Number: 2024944793

Printed in China

First edition

FOREWORD

First of all, I'm going to say something to you that maybe you've heard a million times over, or maybe not enough: Congratulations!

For most of my twenties and thirties, I attended countless weddings, serving as both a party guest and a top-tier bridesmaid, always wondering if I'd ever have one of my own. (I never let that thought stop me from being first on the dance floor or the reason the open bar ran out of champagne.) When I finally met my Perpetual Plus-One in late 2022, I knew I wanted to spend the rest of my life with him. And *wow*, what a feeling that was!

In a world of seven billion people—where it seems statistically impossible to meet someone who aligns with you in every way worthy of "now and forever"— it's a pretty spectacular feat to fall in love.

Maybe you knew this day would come. Or maybe fate surprised you in the best way possible. Whether you met your partner this year or in another lifetime, whether you're swiftly eloping or having an elaborate celebration with every person you love, whether you're simply bursting with joy about the engagement or in a tizzy about wedding planning, it's important to plant your feet firmly on the ground and breathe deeply— absorb all the beauty amidst the chaos of this bridal era. Inhale the romance, the charm, the excitement, the togetherness. Exhale the nerves, the stress, the variables, the uncertainties. (Repeat this exercise until further notice.)

Being a bride feels like you're a perfectly taut white satin bow holding a bouquet of a million emotions. (Don't worry, it's okay to come a little untied!) After some breathwork, take inventory—of your bandwidth, your budget, your mental health, and your priorities. (This is peak self-care!) And as you inch closer and closer to the big day, center yourself with the reminder of *why* you're embarking on such a stunning milestone.

Speaking as someone who revels in the promise of an epic celebration—the contagious party energy, the bottomless champagne, the decadent cake, the fantastic outfits, the heartwarming toasts, the love and passion and joy radiating from every corner of the room—I found it vital to remember that while my odds-defying love deserved a grand presentation, the lifelong commitment to myself and to my partner was at the heart of it all.

Before you said yes to the dress (or any other wedding garment), you said yes to chance, to hope, to possibility, to unimaginable love, and most importantly, to yourself. A wedding is not just a commemoration of two people in love—it's a celebration of all the moments in life that led up to this one and all the incredible moments yet to come.

A few wishes for you: With so much tradition at play, I hope you embrace nontradition where it suits you. I hope you are showered with a surplus of love from start to finish and beyond. I hope you walk by any mirror in your current exact form and think, *I look like a bride*. And I hope, more than anything, that your wedding day is just one of a thousand days in this lifetime you get to say, "Best day ever!"

Enjoy the ride, bride. And let this book be your guide through it all. Congratulations again.

BEFORE *I DO*

"Know your own happiness.
You want nothing but
patience—or give it a more
fascinating name, call it hope."

—Jane Austen,
Sense and Sensibility

CONGRATULATIONS! YOU'RE ENGAGED.

You can't wait to tell everyone: You get to spend the rest of your life with your best friend.

Before long, though, it all starts to weigh on you: the family drama, the endless to-do lists, the decision fatigue, the expectations about what your wedding "should" be.

It doesn't have to be this way. You can be a balanced, healthier version of you, full of confidence as you approach your wedding day and finally walk down the aisle.

This book helps you in your journey to self-care—during wedding planning, at the ceremony, and ever after.

Imagine yourself at your ten-, twenty-, or fifty-year wedding anniversary. What will you remember about your wedding? What will really matter?

You might remember your first dance, the glimmer of tears in your partner's eyes. Maybe your eighty-year-old grandma got up on the dance floor and rocked out with the band. Or your maid of honor gave a speech that made you laugh and cry.

You will probably remember that feeling of elation as you and your partner walk back down the aisle after saying "I do," looking out at all your cheering loved ones. Perhaps the two of you managed to steal a quiet moment together—a look, a kiss, a whisper of reassurance.

You probably *won't* remember the font you used on the invitations, the centerpiece that wasn't quite straight, or the missing garter that you forgot to pack.

Your memories will be about the people. The way they made you feel.

Focus on that. Focus on that *now*.

A wedding does not need to be a performance for the guests attending. Above all, it's a celebration of love and a joyful gathering.

Think back to the last wedding you attended. Do you remember the emotions, the joy, and the celebration . . .

. . . or the cake topper and
the chairbacks at the reception?
We always think the details
matter more than they do.

Develop a plan, create a budget, and then stick to them. Trust that you and your partner can do this.

SAY THIS OUT LOUD:

I release all worries
about what could go wrong
on my wedding day.

When your to-do list feels overwhelming, it's probably time to delegate. Friends and family want to help. Give a trusted loved one a job, and then *let it go.*

Perhaps you are feeling fatigued from decision-making. What kind of cake topper do you want? Do you need ring pillows? Will you have a flower girl? Band or DJ? Which of these things *truly matter to you*? And what can you let go of? Prioritize. Pick what feels important and focus on that.

Less can be more.

Ditch the traditions,
expectations, trends, and DIY
projects that don't serve you.

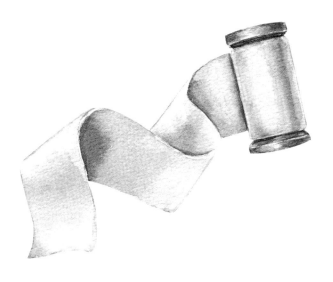

Invite-list decisions can be tough. Are you including kids? Plus-ones? For peace of mind, communicate your expectations with guests clearly and early.

SAY THIS OUT LOUD:

I am confident that I will
plan the wedding that is right
for me and my partner.

Allow your mother-in-law to have control over one thing.

There are no rules to follow. It's *your* wedding. You can offer doughnuts instead of wedding cake, have a taco bar instead of serving salmon, or throw a polka dance party instead of doing the electric slide.

Take one day a week where you don't do anything wedding-related. Go on a walk, have a nice dinner with your partner or friends, and *don't talk about the wedding.*

Your wedding attire does need to be in budget, but it *doesn't* have to match anyone else's vision or style.

Choose to wear what will make you feel like *you* and radiate self-confidence.

Emotions can run high
during wedding planning.

You may feel the weight
of family drama, and the
unsolicited opinions from
others on how the wedding
"should" go and who "should"
be invited may seem endless.

Take a deep breath.

Remember, your wedding is supposed to be a beautiful time for you to reflect on this relationship with someone you love. You don't need to worry so much about what other people are going to think.

You don't have to lose weight or look a certain way for your wedding—you are loved just as you are.

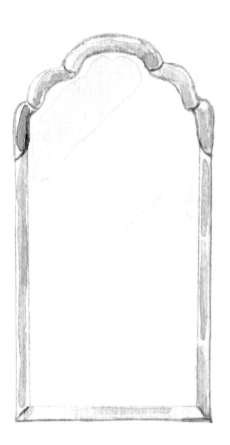

affirmation

Our wedding day will
be filled with joy and love.

Your wedding doesn't have to be like your friends' or frenemies' receptions, the ones who planned a TikTok–worthy first dance or an elaborate bridal party entrance.

Comparing—especially
on social media—will only
make you miserable.

Bridesmaid conflicts? Family drama? Take plenty of time to cool off before a calm, direct discussion. Acknowledge how the other person feels and then focus on solutions. Be firm but kind—it's *your* wedding, and you don't want any long-term damage to friendships or other relationships.

Write vows early—use them as a touchstone for the months to come.

Talk to your partner
about your worries.

Sometimes just saying
how you feel out loud will
help you release the emotions
and begin to feel better.

Don't forget that *you chose this.* You can also choose to scrap plans and elope. You and your partner get to decide what works best for your lives.

affirmation

I am grateful for the support
of friends and family.

Remember that anxiety about the wedding is not the same as anxiety about the marriage.

Try to do things with
your partner that don't
include wedding planning
to keep yourself grounded
in the relationship.

If it feels like too much to plan
a honeymoon and a wedding
at the same time, remember
that a honeymoon can come
a month or two—even a
year—after the wedding.

Write vows to yourself, too. Yes, you are marrying your partner, and you will vow your love and loyalty to them, but in order to show up as the best spouse you can be, you also need to show up for yourself. How will you commit to your self-care now, during wedding planning? How will you commit to your self-care after the wedding? Throughout your marriage?

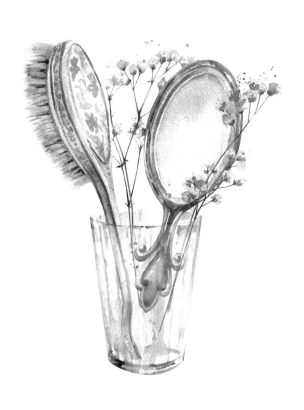

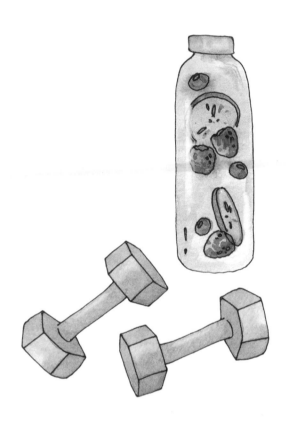

What are your top three self-care habits—the actions you can take that make a big difference in your day? Exercising? Getting enough sleep? Journaling? Meditating? Spending quality time with friends?

Self-care looks different for everyone, but being consistent with your top three habits will alleviate the wedding planning stress and improve your overall well-being.

SAY THIS OUT LOUD:

I am thankful for my
partner and the strength
of our relationship.

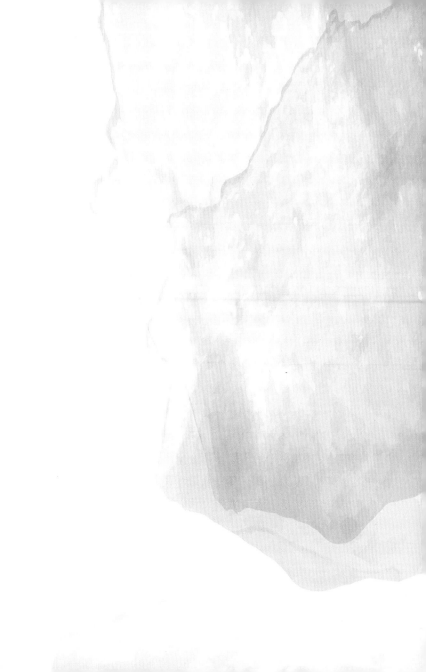

Laughter is therapeutic.

Find levity where you can.

Maybe you just *can't* find
humor in something stressful
about wedding planning.

That's okay.

Take a break from the problem and set aside time to watch a movie that makes you laugh, listen to a stand-up comic, or hang out with a funny friend.

Create a calm-down playlist and a pump-up playlist. Yes, both! You'll want at-the-ready songs that remind you of romantic moments with your partner and help you chill out. And you will want confidence-boosting anthems to belt out with your bridal party.

SAY THIS OUT LOUD:

I free myself from anxiety.
I breathe in positive energy.

Treat yourself.

Self-care starts from within,
but sometimes you need to
stop and indulge—draw a
warm bath, try a face mask,
eat some really great chocolate,
or get a professional massage.

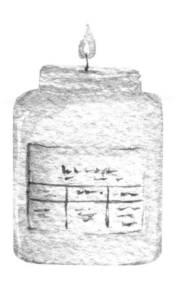

Consider meditation. Set a timer, get comfortable, close your eyes, and focus on your breath. Then relax each muscle in your body, from your toes all the way to your forehead. Breathe.

Make time for creativity.

Drawing, writing, dancing—
creativity breaks will help fuel
you when your wedding
to-do list seems like drudgery.

Journal. Reflect on this
happy moment, the journey
to your wedding day, and
your hopes for the future.

Breathe.

Sleep.

affirmation

SAY THIS OUT LOUD:

I am ready
for the next chapter.

"We can only love others
as much as we love ourselves."

—Brené Brown,
The Gifts of Imperfection

ON THE WEDDING DAY

"What greater thing is there for two human souls, than to feel that they are joined for life—to strengthen each other in all labor, to rest on each other in all sorrow, to minister to each other in all pain, to be one with each other in silent unspeakable memories at the moment of the last parting?"

—George Eliot,
Adam Bede

You want to spend your
life with this person.

And this person wants to spend their life with you.

Pause on that.

affirmation

I am beautiful
exactly as I am.

This day doesn't have to be perfect. No day is perfect.

But it will be beautiful.

Remember: Your relationship
is what matters—the wedding
is just the cherry on top.

SAY THIS OUT LOUD:

I will focus on what matters
on my wedding day.

Before the day begins, try
loving-kindness meditation.

Close your eyes and wish
yourself happiness and love,
then visualize your partner and
wish them happiness and love.

Then visualize all your wedding
guests and wish them all
happiness and love. Observe
how this exercise makes you feel.

There is no perfect weather.
You can't control the weather. If
it rains, embrace it. If nothing
else, it will be memorable!

When things don't go to plan,
you'll get a great story for later.

SAY THIS OUT LOUD:

I am loved exactly as I am.

Nobody will care if things aren't perfect—they are there to celebrate *you* and your partner, not for the free food.

Ask for help on your
wedding day.

People want to help make your day beautiful because they love you. It makes them feel important and gives them a chance to show you how much they love you. They want you to enjoy your day.

SAY THIS OUT LOUD:

I will show my love
and appreciation for my
partner every day.

Designate someone else to receive any day-of updates or complications and give them decision-making power.

Let them filter out any info that you don't truly need so you can just enjoy the day.

"Live now. . . . Catch the beauty of the moment!"

—Leo F. Buscaglia,
Love: What Life Is All About

affirmation

SAY THIS OUT LOUD:

I am surrounded by love.

Have a safe word. And when someone in your inner circle hears you say it, they:

a) pull you away from a long
conversation you're having
with a chatty relative

b) bring you something
to eat, or

c) bring you a drink.

Dance!

affirmation

SAY THIS OUT LOUD:

I love my partner deeply.

Your wedding day is *not* the most beautiful you'll ever look or the happiest you'll ever be.

It's just the beginning.

In the unknown is also
the joy that you didn't
know was possible.

SAY THIS OUT LOUD:

We will create a beautiful
life together.

"Being deeply loved by
someone gives you strength,
while loving someone
deeply gives you courage."

—Lao Tzu

WEDDING COLORS
FOR CALM

RESOURCES

WEBSITES AND ARTICLES FROM THE WEB

"10 Easy Self-Care Strategies to Help You Manage
Stress" by Elizabeth Scott
www.verywellmind.com/importance-of-self-care-for
-health-stress-management-3144704

Bridechilla: Helping You Ditch Wedding Stress and
Plan the Wedding You Want
www.thebridechilla.com

The Gottman Institute (relationship guidance)
www.gottman.com

"How to Manage Wedding Stress" by Sanjana Gupta
www.verywellmind.com/wedding-stress-causes
-symptoms-and-coping-strategies-6741878

"How to Strengthen Loving Relationships with Mindfulness"
www.mindful.org/how-to-be-mindful-in-love

"Need a Breather? Try These 9 Breathing Exercises to Relieve Anxiety" by Sheryl Ankrom
www.verywellmind.com/abdominal-breathing-2584115

"Why I'm not Losing Weight for My Wedding" by Sara K. Runnels
betches.com/wedding-planning-not-losing-weight

APPS

Calm (for sleep, anxiety, and meditation)
www.calm.com

Headspace (for meditation)
www.headspace.com

Trello (for planning)
trello.com

PODCASTS

The Bridal Wellness Podcast: Self-Care for the Bride-to-Be

Whispers to a Bride: Emotional Insight for Your Wedding Drama

BOOKS

Fight Right: How Successful Couples Turn Conflict into Connection by Julie Schwartz Gottman, PhD, and John Gottman, PhD

How to Love by Thich Nhat Hanh

The Gifts of Imperfection by Brené Brown

ABOUT THE
FOREWORD AUTHOR

SARA K. RUNNELS is a humorist, creative writer, copywriter, and screenwriter living in Seattle, Washington. She's a regular humor contributor to *The New Yorker*, with notable work featured in *ELLE*, *Cosmopolitan*, *McSweeney's*, *Betches*, and *Overheard*, among other publications that respect scintillating wordplay and bleeding-heart narratives. Her witticisms, viral one-liners, and sharp social commentary about modern dating, relationships, and simply existing in unprecedented times can be found, quite literally, all over the internet under the handle @omgskr.

The gift of self-care is important
in all life stages—check out all the titles
in the A Little Book of Self-Care series:

A Little Book of Self-Care for Those Who Grieve

A Little Book of Self-Care for the College-Bound

A Little Book of Self-Care for Brides